Why trial for Oklahoma in LA + these men in Miami?

WITH HONOR, COURAGE AND PRIDE

DEFENSE STATEMENTS AT THE SENTENCING HEARINGS OF THE FIVE CUBAN PATRIOTS UNJUSTLY CONDEMNED BY A MIAMI FEDERAL COURT

D1450428

Printing Office of the Cuban Council of State
Havana, 2002

ISBN 959-7030-58-6

First edition: February, 2002
Second edition: March, 2002

Oficina de Publicaciones del Consejo de Estado de la República de Cuba, calle 17 número 552, esquina a D, Vedado, La Habana, Cuba tel: (537)55-1786 / fax: (537)57-4578 / e-mail: palvarez@ip.etecsa.cu

CONTENTS

A SUN THAT WILL NEVER BURN OUT[1]

Early in the morning of Saturday, September 12, 1998, the FBI informed Ileana Ros-Lehtinen and Lincoln Díaz Balart, hornblowers for the Batistian terrorist mob in Miami, that it had just arrested five purported "spies" living there.

Although the Florida Congressional Delegation comprises 25 individuals, none of the others were given advance notice by the investigators. At the time, the FBI had yet to ascertain the identity of three of the men arrested, while the other two held U.S. citizenship. The above-mentioned "legislators" do not occupy positions in Congress related to security or intelligence matters. Why this privilege? Why share information with them from an "investigation" yet to be made public?

Formal charges were not laid until four days later. But from the very beginning, it was clear that this was a case of a political-repressive operation, aimed solely at benefiting the most aggressive and violent sector of those who had

---

[1] Introduction to the book published by the Colombia-Cuba Friendship Association, containing the statements made by Gerardo Hernández, Ramón Labañino, Fernando González, Antonio Guerrero and René González at their sentencing hearings in Miami.

turned South Florida into the main base for their war on Cuba since 1959.

The various counterrevolutionary factions and politicians and officials closely tied to them immediately unleashed a frenzied and hysterical campaign to stigmatize the five prisoners. There in South Florida, where almost all of the printed, radio and television media are controlled by the anti-Cuban mob or operate under its constant threat, not a day went by without the appearance of new articles or announcements, including statements by officials, slandering and denigrating the five by portraying them as dangerous enemies of society.

The real reason behind their unjust imprisonment was hidden. Not a word was published about the unblemished and honorable trajectory of their exemplary lives, in Cuba and the United States, as students, workers, fathers or citizens. Nothing was said about the selfless and admirable sacrifices they made to protect their country and its people. Nor was anything said about what had happened to them since the early morning hours of that September 12, or about the brutal conditions they suffered in one of the worst prison systems ever even imagined by humankind.

Gerardo Hernández, Ramón Labañino, Fernando González, Antonio Guerrero and René González are victims of an abominable injustice and of cruel, inhuman and degrading treatment that blatantly violates their human rights and is irrefutable proof of the arbitrariness and illegitimacy of the legal proceedings to which they were submitted. From the day of their arrest until February 3, 2000, throughout 17 months, they were kept in solitary *confinement, isolated from each other and from other prisoners. They were shut up the entire time in the "hole", a term used to describe the unspeakable treatment reserved for part of the U.S. prison population. The legal representation for the five fought tenaciously until the men were finally integrated into the regular prison system. But the fact that this was accomplished in no way diminishes the unjustifiable atrocity committed against them. What is more, their treatment constituted a violation of U.S. prison regulations, which establish the use of solitary confinement solely as punishment for infractions committed in prison, and limit its length to a maximum of 60 days for the most serious cases, such as murder. They had obviously not violated any of the prison's regulations before being imprisoned, nor had they ever killed anyone. Nevertheless, they were kept in total isolation, and it is worth reiterating, throughout **17 months**.*

During this lengthy period, it was impossible for them to maintain adequate communication with their attorneys and prepare their defense with the minimum guarantees of due process. If there were anything similar to justice in Miami, then for this sole fact, the court should have ordered their release and obliged the government to make adequate reparations.

But in Miami, when it is a matter of Cuba, there is nothing that even remotely resembles justice.

We should mention the commendable work done, in spite of everything, by the defense. The five defendants did not have attorneys of their own, nor the financial resources needed to hire them. As a result, they were assigned public defenders, with whom they had no prior relationship whatsoever. When these lawyers came to know the men they were defending, however, they were able to appreciate the purity of their motivations and the nobility and heroism of their conduct. And despite the profound ideological differences separating them – which they attested to in court – they became convinced of the absolute innocence of the five, as reflected in the personal effort they made to defend them, above and beyond their professional skill.

While the five heroes endured in the shadows and in utter solitude, their cowardly enemies occupied cameras, microphones and newspapers day and night to slander them and threaten their families and friends, as well as to administer "justice" Miami-style. You could read up on all the details of this so-called legal trial in the city's slander sheets, including the details of additional charges that the prosecution would formulate many months later. This was how news came out, for example, of the most aberrant, absurd and false accusation of all – conspiracy to commit murder – presented for the first time by the prosecution in May of 1999. This took place after the prisoners had already spent eight months in jail in complete isolation, and following a shameful operation in the Batistian terrorist mob-controlled press and public and private meetings between the prosecutors and mob members, at which plans to put forward the fallacious charge were openly announced.

Holding a trial in this city with even the appearance of a normal legal proceeding was inconceivable. That it was impossible had been fully demonstrated even before jury selection. Yet the repeated requests made by the defense to have the trial moved to another city were turned down by

Joan Lenard, the Miami federal judge to whom the case was assigned.

During that same time, an event took place that earned notoriety in the international press. Concerned over openly announced threats of violent acts, the organizers of the Latin Grammy Awards decided to move the ceremony originally scheduled to take place in Miami to Los Angeles. If it was not possible to judge the work of some of Cuba's finest musical performers in peace in Miami, if they could not guarantee the safety of the participants in a concert there, as was publicly stated by the organizers, then who could possibly believe that a peaceful and impartial trial could be held there for individuals subjected to the most ferocious slander campaign imaginable and portrayed as "dangerous" agents of the Cuban Revolution?

Ms. Lenard offered no explanation as to why the trial had to be held there, only there, and nowhere else. But she did say something to the press that could provide the key to understanding her stubborn insistence: "this trial will be much more interesting than any TV program," *she proclaimed, erudite and severe, on March 16, 2000.*

Of course, local television turned out to be indispensable for following the trial. It is only fair to acknowledge that the designated counsel responsible for the defense were not locked up in the "hole" *along with the defendants, and unlike the latter, they were allowed to read newspapers, watch television and listen to the radio. We must also point out, however, that it was often through these media that the lawyers received news, long before any official communication was made, of the steps being taken by the prosecution, the purported "evidence" they claimed to possess, the charges that could be laid, and even the motions they raised in their obstinate efforts to introduce some semblance of legality into the midst of such arbitrariness and fraud.*

And if all of the foregoing were not sufficient, there were numerous violations of procedure during the court sessions that even further vitiated a trial that was rigged and therefore nullified from the very outset. The defense attorneys were not allowed access to all of the "evidence" used to back the charges made. Instead, it was selectively doled out by the prosecution, which on more than one occasion introduced hundred of pages of new "evidence" without prior notice, or prevented the complete examination of the documents submitted, leading to repeated objections from the defense. The defense was denied its request for the inclusion of evidence, including official documents, that were fundamental for shedding light on the accusations made against the defendants. A number of witnesses were openly pressured by the prosecution, in front of the judge, right in the courtroom, in view of everyone, under the threat of being charged themselves if they revealed certain information. The court provided the counterrevolution's mouthpieces with over 1400 pages of documents selected by the authorities which was blatantly manipulated by the local press and thus served to fuel the incessant and spurious propaganda campaign to demonize the accused. The media joined with the terrorist groups that freely operate there to organize public demonstrations as a means of pressuring the jury and the judge.

10

That is because, in spite of everything, the mob came to be seriously worried over the way the trial was unfolding. Fully aware of the absolute falseness of the charges made, they feared a verdict contrary to their purposes. They were particularly alarmed by the fact that the defense attorneys, through their talent and high degree of professionalism, had exposed the shady maneuvers of the prosecution and effectively put the mob itself on trial.

The evidence and arguments put forward by the defense were overwhelming. They clearly demonstrated the terrorist activities carried out from Miami against Cuba and the complicit tolerance exhibited by the U.S. authorities, which make it necessary for the Cuban people to defend themselves through the heroic efforts of men like the accused in the case. They made it abundantly clear that the defendants had not sought out information that would threaten the national security of the United States, and had caused no harm to anyone. Testimony to this effect was provided by officials from the FBI itself and the Southern Command, and high-ranking military figures who had held major positions in the U.S. armed forces. These included General Charles Wilhelm, former head of the Southern Command; General Edward Atkeson, former US Army deputy chief of staff intelligence; Rear Admiral Eugene Carroll, former assistant deputy chief of naval operations; and Colonel George Bruckner, who had occupied a high-ranking position in the command of the U.S. Air Defense System. Even General James Clapper, former director of the DIA (the intelligence agency of the U.S. Department of Defense), called to testify as an expert witness for the prosecution, acknowledged that the accused had not committed espionage against the United States.

At the end of five months of courtroom battle, in the most difficult and hostile conditions imaginable, the total innocence of Gerardo, Ramón, Fernando, René and Antonio and the guilt of their accusers had been made abundantly clear.

The accused had carried out no espionage activities whatsoever. They had neither obtained nor sought any information related to the security, defense or any other interest of the United States. They had done nothing to cause damage to that country or its citizens. Not a single piece of inculpatory evidence had been put forward. Not a single witness had uphold the charges.

Their selfless efforts had been focused, solely and exclusively, on infiltrating terrorist groups and informing Cuba of these groups' plans for aggression against the island. They never hid this fact. During the trial, it was thoroughly demonstrated that terrorist acts are carried out against Cuba from Florida, and that the U.S. authorities do nothing in response to these acts. As a result, in the exercise of its inalienable right, Cuba is obliged to defend itself from these activities which, as was also clearly demonstrated, have sometimes led to the loss of lives and serious damage for the people of the United States as well.

The most serious accusation, made against Gerardo Hernández – conspiracy to commit murder, in connection with the incident of February 24, 1996 – is a colossal outrage and unprecedented stupidity. There is a lengthy record of the use of light aircraft taking off from Miami to carry out countless and repeated violations of Cuban airspace and to perpetrate numerous crimes, including shootings, bombings, and the dropping of chemical and bacteriological substances. All of this was amply documented during the trial. It was equally documented that before the date in question, Cuba had warned that it would not tolerate further incursions into its territory. Cuba's defensive action against those who had once again violated its airspace, and right in front of the center of its capital, fully complies with international law. And independently of all of this, Gerardo had nothing to do with the decision carried out by the Cuban air force. He had no involvement whatsoever, in any way, with what happened that day. Consequently charging him with first degree murder and sentencing him to a second life sentence is quite simply the height of both outrage and stupidity. Never before in the history of the US had anyone been found guilty of first degree murder without a single witness, without a shred of proof, without putting forward even circumstantial evidence.

The terrorist mob, in despair, publicly acknowledged its defeat and intensified its virulent and strident campaign to intimidate the court as the trial drew ever closer to its end.

This was the setting in which the jury pronounced its decision. After announcing, with unheard of precision, the exact date and time at which this decision would be pronounced, with remarkable speed, in just a few hours, without asking a single question or expressing a single doubt, it reached a unanimous verdict: the five were declared guilty of each and every one of the charges against them.

A brief aside on the subject of the jury is called for. Right from the time of the jury selection process, its members were subjected to the relentless pressures and maneuvers typical of the poisoned atmosphere of a city totally devoid of lawfulness. The counterrevolution's mouthpieces did not even attempt to hide it. On December 2, 2000, for example, El Nuevo Herald, *in an article entitled "Fear of being jury member in trial of spies",* stated: "The fear of a violent reaction on the part of the Cuban exile community if a jury decides to acquit the five men accused of spying for the island regime has led many potential candidates to ask the judge to excuse them from civic duty." *And one of these citizens is quoted as saying,* "Yes! I fear for my own safety if the verdict is not to the liking of the Cuban community."

This fear was not unfounded. The members of the jury lived in a community that had only recently suffered months of violence and anxiety, when a group of criminals held Elian Gonzalez, a six-year-old boy kidnapped, openly and publicly, defying the federal authorities with firearms. These individuals had burned the American flag, destroyed property, plunged the streets into chaos and threatened to burn the city down, without one of them ever facing trial for these acts. The members of the jury were also aware of the physical and verbal attacks, the threats and bombs used against those who dared to voice opinions contrary to the ones held by those who control this "exile community". If they had done all of these things in broad daylight and in front of television cameras from around the world, what would they not have done in secret to bribe and control a dozen frightened people?

The party got going in the courtroom itself, where prosecutors and mobsters, FBI officials and terrorists merged in a confusing tangle of kisses and embraces. They kept the celebrations going later in bars and taverns and the headquarters of counterrevolutionary organizations, inundating the radio waves, all of them together, with their brazen diatribes and threats against anyone in Miami who opposed these anti-Cuban misdeeds. The head of the local FBI office himself was honored with a public tribute on the local "Cuban radio" stations, which openly advocate war and terrorism on a daily basis; he sang in perfect harmony with the most notorious criminals among them.

In the meantime, the five men were once again locked up in the "hole" from June 26 to August 13. They had committed no infractions whatsoever. There was nothing to justify this new violation of their rights and of prison regulations. It was an act of mindless vengeance to punish them for their integrity, but it was also a form of torture, with the deliberate purpose of breaking them down and preventing them from adequately preparing for the next and final stage of the trial: the sentencing hearings scheduled for the following month. The initial 17 months of solitary confinement were aimed at making it impossible to organize their defense; this further 48 days of complete isolation were meant to prevent them at any cost from preparing for the only opportunity they would have to directly address the court. For this reason, when they were finally returned to their usual cells following insistent demands by their attorneys, their access to telephone communication was restricted and they had most of their belongings taken away,

15

leaving them with barely a pencil stub to write with. First they had tried to make it impossible for them to defend themselves, now they were attempting to stop them from denouncing the crime being committed against them.

Ms. Lenard had originally planned to pronounce judgment during the month of September. But then the atrocious attack on the Twin Towers took place on September 11, and it was perhaps her high degree of sensitivity that led her to allow a suitable amount of time elapse between this date and the tribute that she, as a resident of a Miami herself, would be rendering to the terrorists.

She did it in December. She imposed the toughest sentences possible on all five of the defendants, disregarding the potential mitigating circumstances and incorporating the aggravating circumstances put forward by the prosecution. She essentially acted like an echo of the anti-Cuban hatred and prejudices that had poisoned the entire proceedings, clearly expressing this in words and in the irrationally excessive sentences she passed down. For Gerardo Hernández, **_two life sentences plus 15 years_**; for Ramón Labañino, **_a life sentence plus 18 years_**; for Fernando González, **_19 years in prison_**; for René González, **_15 years in prison_**; and for Antonio Guerrero, **_a life sentence plus 10 years_**.

Yet their voices were not silenced. Their long, brutal and profoundly unjust imprisonment did not intimidate them. Nor were they weakened by the psychological tortures and pressures, or the absence of family and friends. Nothing could break their indomitable spirit. Lacking the basic

16

necessities for organizing their thoughts and getting them down in writing, they were able to rise above the filth that strove to crush them and deliver the formidable statements published in this book.

Far from following the Philistine American tradition of using this final opportunity offered to the accused to grovel before the judges and beg for clemency with a show of repentance, the five men denounced and exposed their accusers, laid bare all of the illegitimacy and arbitrariness of a trial that was fixed from the outset, and reaffirmed their unshakable loyalty to their homeland, their people and their ideals.

At the time these lines were written, the five heroes were once again separated and isolated, newly shut away in some "hole", although their exact location is unknown. All that is known is that Gerardo will be sent to the Lompoc penitentiary in California; Ramón to Beaumont, Texas; Fernando to Oxford, Wisconsin; René to Loreto, Pennsylvania; and Antonio to Florence, Colorado. A quick look at a map of the United States makes it clear that they are being spread to the five most distant and dispersed points in the country possible. As well as distancing them from one another, this arrangement will also make it extremely difficult for them to have any contact with family members living in Cuba and with Cuban diplomatic representatives, who should be allowed access to them, in accordance with international standards.

All five are notoriously severe prisons, to which they undoubtedly send inmates convicted of the worst crimes. Given the potential for brutality demonstrated by the

17

authorities in a place like the federal detention center in Miami, where the five were kept from the time of their arrest along with others awaiting trial, it is easy to imagine the cruelty they will have to endure in the United States' toughest prisons. It is particularly outrageous, and should be denounced as vigorously as possible, that Washington has completely ignored universally accepted principles, standards and practices and failed to acknowledge the political prisoner status of these five heroes of the Republic of Cuba.

The brazenly treacherous conduct of the U.S. authorities in this case fully reveals their genuine stance towards terrorism and the utter hypocrisy of the campaign deployed after the horrific attack of September 11, 2001. These five heroic Cubans are being punished precisely because of the fact that they truly did fight against terrorism, even at the cost of their own lives. Those who have taken away their freedom and sought to slander and denigrate them have done so because they dared to combat the heinous criminals who were created and continue to be protected by those very same authorities. Every hour that they spend locked up in that living hell is an insult to the memory of those who lost their lives on September 11 and all other victims of terrorism. It is also an affront to all those who believe in dignity and human decency. The Cuban people will fight relentlessly until the five are freed and can return to their homes and their homeland. In order to achieve this goal, the solidarity of all men and women of good will around the world is urgently needed.

The five speeches compiled in this book will give the reader an idea of selflessness, nobility and idealism of Gerardo, Ramón, Antonio, Fernando and René.

They are oratory works that will survive the test of time. Millions and millions of people will read them, and feel both moved and grateful. Above and beyond their obvious merits in style and content, they are even more remarkable in view of the terrible circumstances in which they were conceived. They give voice to the very best in all of humankind. They bring a message of struggle, of hope and of victory. They are like a sun whose rays manage to break through the utmost darkness. A sun that will never burn out.

RICARDO ALARCÓN DE QUESADA
President of the National Assembly of People's Power
of the Republic of Cuba

Havana, Cuba, February 11, 2002

DEFENSE STATEMENT PRESENTED BY GERARDO HERNÁNDEZ NORDELO AT THE SENTENCING HEARING

Wednesday, December 12, 2001

Your Honor:

I would like first of all to express a few words of thanks to a number of federal government officials who worked throughout our long and complex trial both inside and outside this courtroom. I am referring to the translators, stenographers, marshals and other assistants, who showed a high professional ethic at all times.

I would also like to publicly express our deepest gratitude to the attorneys who so masterfully represented us, and to all of the people who assisted them in this very difficult task.

So as not to waste your valuable time, I will try to be as brief as possible. There are five defendants in this case, and we share many opinions and views, so I will refrain from referring to important aspects that I know they will want to address in their turn.

Moreover, it would take too much time to point out every one of the inconsistencies of the prosecution and its witnesses, every one of its efforts to use and sometimes manipulate small portions of the evidence while disregarding its larger and more essential significance.

The few minutes I have would not be enough to highlight all of the attempts made by the gentlemen of the prosecution to ensure that the jury was guided more by emotions and prejudices than by the facts and the law; nor would there be enough time to point out every one of the reasons that made this an eminently political trial. Moreover, it might not even be necessary, because no one knows better than you what really happened in this courtroom between December 2000 and June 2001. Nevertheless, there are a number of elements that must not be overlooked.

Those who are not aware of the way the most radical sector of the Cuban community in Miami traditionally operates, those who do not watch Spanish-language television or listen to so-called "Cuban radio", might have sincerely thought that it would be possible for us to be given a fair and impartial trial in this city. Unfortunately, there are many realities of which the U.S. public is still unaware. As for us, from the very moment that we were denied the possibility of having the trial moved out of Miami, we did not have the slightest doubt of what the final outcome would be.

It would be dishonest to deny that as the trial progressed, and in view of the overwhelming arguments and evidence put forward by the defense, combined with the frequently desperate behavior of the prosecution and the reaction of the press, there were moments when we even considered that what seemed to be impossible in this community could perhaps really happen. Yet the jury, with its quick and unequivocal verdict, proved our initial prediction to be accurate. After six months of a complex and exhausting trial, with dozens of testimonies and extensive evidence, the members of the jury needed only a few hours, without even asking a question or voicing a doubt, to reach a unanimous verdict.

It is sufficient to read the statements made to the press by the spokesman of this jury to understand that we never had the slightest chance, and that they were influenced more by prejudices or by the final, deceptive words of the gentlemen of the prosecution than by the arguments they heard here over the course of half a year.

And when I refer to the deceptive behavior of prosecution, I am not making a disrespectful or unfounded accusation. As I said before, there is not enough time to point out every single example. It is enough to recall that the person responsible for translating the majority of the evidence used by the prosecution, an individual who claimed to be an expert in the field, stated before this court that the Spanish word "plastilina" is used to refer to plastic explosives, when in fact, any Hispanic child knows, without being an expert, that the only "plastilina" in our language is what is known in English as "molden clay". Incidentally, the prosecution used the document referring to this "plastilina" over and over again for its alarmist effect, despite knowing, because they do know, that it has nothing to do with any one of the five accused.

It is equally ridiculous that during the trial of people accused of being dangerous spies and a menace to national security, the accusing party has repeatedly stressed an incident that purportedly took place in Cuba, involving a taxi driver from the country's main airport, at a time when the island had just suffered a wave of terrorist attacks. I wonder how many taxi drivers are being watched by the FBI at this very moment in airports across the United States, not only for expressing their discontent with the government, but probably simply for wearing turbans. In order to understand the attitudes of a country or its citizens, it is necessary to live, or suffer, its daily realities. The above-mentioned incident, as inconceivable as it may seem, was even included in the PSI report, although no one could explain what relation it might possibly have to the crimes I have been accused of.

Now that I have mentioned the PSI report, I would like to briefly refer to some of the statements I wrote for the same, and I quote: "Cuba has the right to defend itself from the terrorist acts that are prepared in Florida with total impunity, despite the fact that they have been consistently denounced by the Cuban authorities. This is the same right that the United States has to try to neutralize the plans of terrorist Osama Bin Laden's organization, which has caused so much damage to this country and threatens to continue doing so. I am certain that the sons and daughters of this country who are carrying out this mission are considered patriots, and their objective is not that of threatening the national security of any of the countries where these people are being sheltered." End of quote.

24

This statement was written for the PSI report and sent to my attorney to be translated many days before the tragic and condemnable events of September 11. Today they are more relevant than ever. Just as the president of the United States stated recently before the United Nations, it is necessary for all of the world's countries to unite in the struggle against terrorists, and not against some terrorists, but rather against all terrorists. And I would add that as long as the acts of some of these criminals are condemned, while others are sheltered and allowed to act with impunity against the security and sovereignty of other countries, and considered "freedom fighters", this scourge will never be eradicated. And as long as this is the case, there will always be nations that need to send some of their own people to carry out dangerous missions for their defense, whether it be in Afghanistan or South Florida.

Your Honor, we have been accused of conspiring to commit espionage and harm the national security of the United States. We have been placed on the same level as the worst spies ever known, without a single piece of sound evidence and without having caused any harm whatsoever, solely on the basis of suppositions. Ours may be one of the most ridiculous accusations of espionage in the history of this country. Everything that we intended to do and have done was clearly set out in the evidence put forward. The person who was closest to anything military, after six years of working in his insignificant post, was merely asked to try to find a position that allowed him to be closer to the runways, in order to observe the number of planes. This is not espionage. The evidence and testimony offered by

25

individuals highly qualified in this area have demonstrated that.

On the other hand, it is true that for years, some of we the accused had false identity documents in our possession, but their only purpose was to guarantee our safety. As a judge, you are aware of how many crimes can be committed with false documents, and yet it was acknowledged in this courtroom that the only use made of these documents, when they were used in any way at all, was exclusively aimed at protecting our own personal integrity and that of our families.

Please permit me to briefly refer to what I believe is the reason for which all of us find ourselves here at this moment: the third in the list of charges against us, "conspiracy to commit murder".

The prosecutors and FBI authorities know and knew from the very beginning what truly did take place before, on and after February 24, 1996. They themselves had to acknowledge that the high frequency messages they chose to reveal as evidence are only a minute portion of all the messages they intercepted. They know the true story. They know that there was never any conspiracy to shoot down those planes, much less to do it over international waters. They know perfectly well that not only Gerardo Hernández, but also not even Juan Pablo Roque ever had anything to do with a plot to shoot down the planes. They know that Roque's return had been planned long before for strictly personal reasons, and that in February of 1996, instructions were given for he himself to choose his date of departure, with the recommendation that it be either February 23 or 27, depending upon the availability of airline tickets. If there had been a plot in which Roque was involved, how could he have stayed here until the 27th? This is just one of the many details that make this the most absurd and outrageous of all the charges against us.

After two years of close surveillance, and having taped most of our telephone and personal conversations and confiscated a large quantity of materials from that time period, the prosecutors could not present a single piece of evidence at this trial to demonstrate beyond reasonable doubt that Gerardo Hernández had conspired to shoot down these planes or contributed in a way to this act. They based their entire case on pure speculation, on small excerpts of documents, manipulated and taken out of context, and above all on the emotional and sensitive nature of this accusation, due to the loss of human lives.

It would only be natural to ask what motivated the prosecution to stage its whole propaganda show around this charge, and to seek at any cost to convict someone who they know had nothing to do with the death of those people. The answer is not all that difficult to find. One need only recall the enormous pressure exerted by some sectors of the Cuban community who were not satisfied with the economic sanctions adopted against Cuba following the events of February 24. The repeated accusations made by these individuals and organizations against the government of the United States for its alleged complicity in these events, according to them, and for not doing anything to punish those responsible, became ever more bothersome, just as it was bothersome and unforgivable to these Miami Cubans that the FBI regional office would have infiltrated informers into a number of so-called "exile" organizations, including the "Brothers to the Rescue". It had become necessary to restore images and improve relations, and nothing would work better than finding, or fabricating, a guilty party.

The authorities knew this was a win-win situation. If I was found guilty of the charge, all the better. If I was found innocent, as unlikely as that may have seemed, they would still win, because they could silence those who were accusing them of not having charged anyone.

Perhaps there are people so naive or unaware as to believe that I am exaggerating the importance that some U.S. authorities accord to the opinions and reactions of the most extremist sector of the Cuban community. I would like to remind those people of the fact that the citizens of this nation cannot travel freely to Cuba, or smoke Cuban cigars, or trade in Cuban products without restrictions, or simply immunize their children against diseases for which the only vaccines are patented in Cuba, and further remind them that this fact does not exactly respond to the demands or interests of the American people.

Your Honor, I have always said, and will repeat now, that I deeply regret the loss of those four lives, and I understand the suffering of their families. I also regret the thousands of lives that have been lost as a result of the constant aggression suffered by my people throughout more than 40 years, and the eternal mourning of many, many Cuban families. These dead also have names and faces, although their pictures cannot be shown in this courtroom.

Cuba did not provoke this incident. On the contrary, it foresaw it, and tried to prevent it through every means within its reach. The prosecution's main argument during the trial was that this incident was a crime, because it involved unarmed civilian aircraft. This nation recently found out, in an unfortunate and brutal manner, just how much damage can be done to its people by an unarmed civilian plane. Perhaps that is why its top leaders have warned that any plane that strays threateningly from its scheduled route should be shot down, even if there are hundreds of passengers on board. Perhaps the gentlemen of the prosecution believe this would be a crime. Your Honor said today that this country changed its "perception of danger" after September 11; unfortunately, Cuba had to change its perception of danger on January 1, 1959, and this is what some people fail to understand.

The people primarily responsible for what happened on February 24, 1996 are the same people who do not relent in their efforts to provoke an armed conflict between the United States and Cuba, so that this country's army can do for them what they themselves have not managed to do in 40 years. Be it flotillas, airspace violations, false accusations or any other abomination, the goal is always the same: for the United States to wipe the Cuban government and those who support it off the face of the earth, no matter what the cost in human lives on one side or the other. It can be stated with all certainty that if anyone has repeatedly placed the national security of this country in danger, it has been these extremist Cuban groups.

The prosecution stated in this courtroom, during the final arguments, that Gerardo Hernández has blood on his hands. I wonder whose hands really are stained with blood, if it is me, or the individual who fired a gun on a hotel full of people in Havana, who is the same individual who appears in the evidence of this case planning to smuggle antipersonnel weapons into Cuba; the same person who openly and recklessly defied the Cuban authorities, over and over and over again, violating the laws of that country, the laws of this country, and the most elemental rules of international aviation; the same person who not only did not hesitate to lead these young men to their deaths, but who also, in the moments of greatest tension, when there was still time to go back on his plans, did not do so, and instead left his laughter on tape for all of history, while his comrades were dying.

This person's hands truly are stained with blood, yet this did not seem to matter to the gentlemen of the prosecution when they shook those bloodied hands on numerous occasions, even in this very courtroom. Nor did it matter to the prosecutors or the top FBI authorities in Miami when they shared the stage and the celebrations with this same person during the press conference on the day the verdict was announced. This is rather contradictory behavior for those who claim to represent the law.

I want the gentlemen of the prosecution to know that the only blood there may be on these hands is the blood of my brothers and sisters who have fallen or been cowardly murdered in the countless acts of aggression and terrorism perpetrated against my country by individuals who freely walk the streets of this city today. And it is for this blood that I made the pledge to sacrifice even my own life if doing so could protect my people from such crimes.

Your Honor, the prosecution considers, and has requested, that I should spend the rest of my life in prison. I trust that if not at this level, then at some other level of the system, reason and justice will prevail over political prejudices and the desire for revenge, and it will be understood that we have done no harm to this country that deserves such a punishment. But if this were not the case, I would then take the liberty of quoting one of this nation's greatest patriots, Nathan Hale, when he said: "My only regret is that I have but one life to give for my country."

Thank you very much.

Gerardo Hernández Nordelo

DEFENSE STATEMENT PRESENTED BY RAMÓN LABAÑINO SALAZAR AT THE SENTENCING HEARING

Thursday, December 13, 2001

Your Honor, Ladies and Gentlemen:

First of all, I join in all of the arguments put forward by my four brothers in this case and in my recognition of the professional behavior of the officials in this court: Richard, the translators, the marshals, and Lisa.

The criminal attacks on the Twin Towers in New York and the Pentagon in Washington took the lives of thousands of innocent people in the United States, and we share in the anger and sorrow of the American people. It is our fervent hope that events like these are never repeated.

We who have devoted our lives to fighting terrorism, to preventing atrocious acts like these from taking place; we who have tried to save the lives of innocent human beings not only in Cuba but in the United States as well, stand in this courtroom today to be sentenced precisely for preventing similar acts. Thus, this punishment could not be more ironic and unfair!

The words of George W. Bush, president of this country, in the name of which I am to be sentenced, clearly express the reasons why we came to the United States and why we find ourselves in this courtroom today.

From this very city of Miami, terrorist acts against my country, Cuba, have been planned, organized and directed. From here, the terrorists and their activities are sponsored, encouraged and financed. They are given shelter here as well. To mention just one well-known case, a terrorist and murderer not only of Cubans but of people from the United States as well, Orlando Bosch, freely walks the streets of Miami. And what is most regrettable of all is that all of this takes place with the knowledge and consent of this country's authorities. One need only thoroughly read all of the evidence in our case, which gives a full account of all these kinds of terrorist activities.

Cuba, my country, has suffered more than 42 years of terrorist acts, aggression, invasions and provocations, which have resulted in the deaths of over 3478 innocent human beings and physical injuries to over 2099. Cuba, like the United States, has the right to defend itself.

To offer just a few examples:

On March 4, 1960, the French ship *La Coubre* was blown up in the port of Havana by agents of the CIA; 101 people were killed as a result of this terrorist sabotage, including six French sailors.

On October 6, 1976, in a treacherous terrorist attack perpetrated by Luis Posada Carriles and Orlando Bosch, through Venezuelan mercenaries, two bombs were detonated on a Cubana Airlines civilian aircraft that had taken off from the Barbados, cruelly killing 73 people (57 Cubans, including 24 youths from the Cuban National Fencing Team,

11 young people from Guyana, and five Koreans). Some of these terrorist murderers are in prison today in Panama, and enormous efforts are being made here in Miami to have them set free. Here they are called "patriots" and regarded as symbols; radio stations are raising funds for their defense and possible escape from jail.

There have been 637 attempts on the life of the president of Cuba, Fidel Castro.

Bacteriological terrorism aimed at humans, plants and animals has also been used against my country, with a total of 344,203 people affected and 158 dead, of whom 101 were children.

This is not paranoia, these are lives of innocent human beings!

These terrorist groups we were acting against not only carried out these kinds of activities in Cuba, but also here in the United States. This news report, which is totally public and available to everyone, provides a summary of the terrorist acts committed here in Miami, a total of over 68 acts of violence. This article written by journalist Jim Mullin of the *Miami New Times* on April 20-26, 2000, among many other incidents, reports the following:

1968   Orlando Bosch fires a bazooka from the MacArthur Causeway against a Polish ship (Miami politicians would later declare an "Orlando Bosch Day" to honor this terrorist).

1974   Exile leader José Elías de la Torriente is murdered in Coral Gables for the failure of an invasion he was to lead to Cuba.

1975   Luciano Nieves is murdered after defending peaceful coexistence with Cuba.

1976   Emilio Milán, the news director at WQBA-AM, has his legs blown off by a car bomb after publicly condemning the violence perpetrated by the exile community.

1981   A bomb explodes in the Mexican consulate on Brickell Ave., in protest over Mexico's relations with Cuba.

1996   A bomb explodes in the Little Havana restaurant Centro Vasco, to protest a scheduled concert by Cuban singer Rosita Fornés.

2000   On April 11, outside the home of Elián González' relatives in Miami, radio journalist Scott Piasant of Obregón holds up a T-shirt reading "Send the boy home, it's a father's right", and is physically attacked before the police arrive.

These things did not happen in Cuba. They happened here in the United States, in Miami, in the cities and streets of this country where we all live, where you and your children and families walk every day.

In the 1990s, terrorism, raids and provocations against my country were stepped up, until in 1997 there was a wave of terrorist acts against hotels and other tourism establishments that resulted in the murder of an innocent Italian tourist, Mr. Favio Di Celmo.

How many more deaths of innocent human beings must we witness before this insane and absurd policy towards Cuba is ended?

How many more human lives must be lost before the FBI truly fulfills its duty and arrests the real criminals and terrorists who act against the people of the United States itself?

Could it be that this "fight against terrorism" is pure rhetoric?

No, common sense would say that it is not. And that is precisely why we are here today, because we do not want any of these things to happen, neither in Cuba, nor in the United States, or Miami, or any other part of the world. All that we have done is this: to try to save the lives of innocent human beings, by preventing terrorism and preventing a stupid war.

The same pattern can be observed in all of the Cuban-American terrorists we know. José Basulto was recruited and trained by the CIA and used in its war against my country, and he has kept up the practice of terrorism and provocation up until today, just like the members of such organizations as the Cuban-American National Foundation, Alpha 66, Comandos F-4, the Democratic National Unity Party (PUND), Independent and Democratic Cuba (CID), and the many others referred to in our evidence. These terrorists represent to Cuba what the perpetrators of the horrific acts committed against the United States represent to this country.

Cuba has never trusted these characters, and it never will. Nor should the United States trust them, much less protect them. This is a serious mistake, which could explain in part why events like those of September 11 happen.

My country has suffered from terrorism for more than 42 years. Today the United States is suffering, and if this problem is not eradicated at the root, it could continue to suffer tomorrow. Here in the United States there are more than 800 organizations of a violent nature; this country is the one most vulnerable to these kinds of criminal acts. Terrorism is the true enemy of the national security of the United States. Maintaining a stance of inactivity or indifference, or worse yet, of complicity and concealment of terrorists and terrorism, is the worst crime that can be committed against the national security of this nation; and that is precisely what is happening in this case. Those who protect these groups and individuals are the ones really endangering the national security of the United States.

And that is why, from this forum, I denounce the law enforcement agencies of the United States that have concealed and failed to take action against terrorism and terrorists!

For many years, Cuba has passed information on to various government agencies in the United States, up to the highest level; detailed, documented information, complete with names and conclusive evidence of criminal acts and murders. Our own evidence in this case is a full sampling of that information. And even with all this information in their hands, they have done nothing. There has not been a single arrest, or even a single investigation carried out or underway.

With our arrest, all they have attempted to do is to silence the source of information, to keep serious acts of terrorism like these from disclosure and to hide the truth that so brutally hits us today. Moreover, the FBI has conspired with the terrorists themselves and the extreme right wing in Miami to damage and obstruct any kind of rapprochement and cooperation between our two peoples and governments. Meanwhile, the criminals are happily walking the streets outside here today, laughing at this courtroom. There cannot be a greater offense or stain on these authorities, on the flag presiding this courtroom, and on that coat-of-arms representing the ideal of true justice.

All that Cuba wants is to live in peace and tranquillity. It does not want a war, just as the people of the United States do not want a war. The military leaders of the United States do not want it either, because they know very well that Cuba poses no danger whatsoever to this country. That is why our work has also been aimed at preventing a criminal war, which would only lead to the deaths of innocent people, not only from Cuba, but also from the United States.

At no time have we sought out information that could place the national security of this country in danger. This is pure manipulation, which we will never accept, and a reason for which we decided to come to this trial, in addition to clearly exposing the truth about all of the criminal acts perpetrated from U.S. territory against Cuba and the United States itself.

It is not Cuba that has come to the United States for the purpose of an invasion, aggression, or terrorist acts of all kinds. The reality is the complete opposite, and quite simply, Cuba has the basic right to defend itself. That is all that we have done, without causing harm to anyone or anything.

As long as this criminal policy against my people persists, there will continue to be men like us, as a basic measure of self-defense, just as the United States urgently needs to learn about the inner workings of the terrorist organizations attacking it today. This is a reality that no one can bring to an end.

What the members of the Miami extreme right are really seeking is to create a conflict through some sort of provocation that will result in a U.S. military attack against Cuba. And as I have said, this is not what my people, or my government, or the people of the United States want. General Sheehan's testimony regarding the infiltrations into Cuba by Ramón Saúl Sánchez and his "Democracy" group, revealed that he did not want these elements to provoke a war with Cuba, which could cost the lives of many young men in the U.S. armed forces. Numerous similar points of view were expressed in this courtroom.

As for the prosecution, we have seen a truly shameful and reprehensible behavior that has nothing to do with justice and the search for truth. They first tried to suppress all of our evidence on the terrorist acts perpetrated both in Cuba and here in the United States. They used every means possible to try to suppress 90% of our evidence in this case, that is, the truth about our mission here.

The prosecutors have manipulated and distorted the facts. They have tried to control this courtroom at all times. They have used both subtle and blatant threats. They have resorted to blackmailing witnesses under the threat of legally incriminating them if they did not plead the Fifth Amendment. They even went so far as to try to blackmail four-star General Charles Whilhem, former chief of the Southern Command, to stop him from testifying for the defense.

There have been attempts to conceal evidence (an 8 mm video, when FBI agent Al Alonso prevented the original from being turned over to the defense; this was a key piece of evidence for the most serious charge in this case).

For us, the prosecutors do not represent the government of the United States, and that is why for us, this is not a case of the Government of the United States vs. Gerardo Hernández. Actually, the prosecution has very skillfully represented the small extremist right-wing sector of the Cuban community, terrorists like José Basulto and organizations like Alpha 66, the Cuban-American National Foundation and Comandos F-4. They even went so far as to embrace and kiss these individuals right in this courtroom, in full view of everyone here. If something about this trial astonished me, it was the tremendous zeal, the unlimited efforts made by the prosecution and all their advisors to faithfully represent this criminal sector, at any cost.

However, the defense has showed truth, dignity and the real stance of the American people towards Cuba. It was the defense that brought in generals and other military and civilians who have contributed to carrying out this policy towards my country, such as:

General Charles Whilhem
Admiral Atkinson
Colonel Eugene Carol

Colonel Buckner

Richard Nuccio, former advisor to U.S. President William Clinton on Cuban affairs.

Many of them appeared on a fully voluntary basis, and in this small detail lies a very big message for those willing to understand it.

Ladies and gentlemen: this is a time of major changes; we are well into the 21st century. Today the United States has relations with China. It has relations with Viet Nam, where 56,000 citizens of this country died. It is taking part in talks with North Korea, and many other countries with which it seemed impossible to have relations. Why not with Cuba?

It is true that to carry out our tasks, we needed to resort to unconventional methods. We have done so for obvious reasons of personal security, and never with the intent of harming anyone, or cheating or deceiving anyone, much less the government or institutions of this country.

The evidence is overwhelmingly clear in all respects, then, let us be judged on the basis of that evidence. From the very first day of this trial, we acknowledged our true identities and our responsibilities, but I never accepted, and never will accept, any implication of espionage, or of trying to deceive this country.

I want to express special thanks for the work of our attorneys, for their courage and professionalism. For us, and for everyone, we have won this trial. History will take care of rectifying this verdict, and perhaps this sentence as well.

Gentlemen of the prosecution, whether you like it or not, Cuba is an independent and sovereign country. It has its own legitimate government, its own president, its own martyrs and heroes, and its own convictions. Cuba is not different from the United States. And, gentlemen, Cuba must be respected!

We know that efforts were made to ensure an impartial trial. But the city of Miami is not a place where goals like these can be achieved when it comes to Cuba. Perhaps that was the most critical error in our case: holding the trial in this city.

If preventing the deaths of innocent human beings, defending our two countries from terrorism, and preventing a senseless invasion of Cuba is the reason I am being sentenced today, then, let that sentence be welcomed.

I will wear the prison uniform with the same honor and pride with which a soldier wears his most prized insignia.

This has been a political trial, therefore, we are political prisoners.

All of the evidence is here; this is where history is written. And it is history that will do us true justice.

Thank you.

Ramón Labañino Salazar

STATEMENT PRESENTED BY RENÉ GONZÁLEZ SEHWERERT AT THE SENTENCING HEARING

Friday, December 14, 2001

Before I begin, I would like to propose an experiment to those present in the courtroom today: close your eyes, and imagine that you are in downtown New York. Now, when the first firefighter comes along, look him straight in the eye, very seriously, and tell him to his face that nothing happened on September 11. That it is all a lie. Nothing but camera tricks. It is all pure paranoia and propaganda. At this point, if neither your own shame, nor the poor firefighter, has made you swallow your words, then you are eminently qualified to have been a prosecutor in this case.

And now, with the permission of this Court, I will begin.

Your Honor:

Months ago, in one of her efforts to sweep the subject of terrorism against Cuba under the carpet, using the twisted logic of her confused argument on intent and motivation,

Mrs. Heck Miller told the court that we could leave the political speeches until this point in the trial. Even back then, when all of the prosecutors' political hatred had been unleashed on us through the conditions of our confinement, the manipulation of the evidence, and, even worse, the use and abuse of my own family to blackmail, hurt and humiliate me, I was far from imagining just how important it would be for the prosecution in this case to pour out all of their political rancor towards us.

Nevertheless, after six months of listening to these same prosecutors shoving their prejudices down the jury's throats over and over again, I can still tell Mrs. Heck Miller that she was wrong. I do not need to speak of my political beliefs, which I do not in any way renounce, to say that I condemn terrorism, that I condemn war, and that I feel profound contempt for those people, so completely obsessed with their hatreds and petty interests, who have devoted so much time to harming their country by promoting terrorism and fostering a war on which they squander all the courage that they do not have and that others will need, also their victims, on the battlefield.

I do not need to talk politics, to say that I believe that innocent people should not have to die for this, neither in Cuba, nor here in the United States, nor anywhere else in the world. And I would do what I did and take the risks that I took for any country in the world, including the United States, regardless of political considerations.

I firmly believe that you can be a Catholic and be a good person, that you can be a Jew and be a good person, that you can be a capitalist, a Muslim or a communist and be a good person; but there is no such thing as a good person who is also a terrorist. You must be sick to be a terrorist, just as you must be sick to believe that there is such a thing as a good terrorist.

Unfortunately, not everyone feels the same way. When it comes to Cuba, the rules apparently change, and some people think that terrorism and war are good things to do. And so we have a prosecutor like Mr. Kastrenakes who defends José Basulto's right to break the law as long as it is announced on television. We have an expert on terrorism like Mr. Hoyt, who believes that ten explosions in a one-year period would constitute a wave of terrorism in Miami, but not in Havana. We have an air safety expert for whom the acts of provocation perpetrated by Brothers to the Rescue against Havana, widely publicized on television, would be a different thing if they were perpetrated against Washington, because they would be, according to him, more urgent and verifiable. We have people who for 40 years have publicly advertised themselves as terrorists, yet the prosecutors to my left only seem to have noticed it when they testified in this case for the defense. Agents Angel Berlinguerí and Héctor Pesquera, the latter no less than the head of the local FBI, proudly appear as guests on the same radio stations, with the same people and on the same programs that violate federal laws by openly raising funds to organize terrorist activities or defend terrorists around the world.

Meanwhile, Mrs. Caroline Heck Miller calls for these nice terrorists to be judged in heaven, while Mr. Frómeta, after trying to buy nothing more than a couple of surface-to-air missiles, antitank weapons and a bit of highly potent explosive, is considered a good father, a good citizen and a good person, who might deserve something like a year of house arrest from the South Florida District Attorney's Office. This, your Honor, as far as I know, is called hypocrisy, and it is also criminal.

And when this same office fights to keep me in a Special Housing Unit for as long as possible, when my family is used as an instrument to break my will, when my daughters are only allowed to see their father twice during the 17 months of this isolation and the only way I can watch the first steps taken by my little girl is through a 12th floor window, then I can only feel proud of being here, and I can only thank the prosecutors for giving me this opportunity to confirm that I am on the right track, that the world still needs a lot of improving, and that the best thing for the people of Cuba is to keep the island clean of the element that has taken over so many souls here in Miami. I want to thank them for allowing me to prove myself against their hatred and resentment, and for this pride I feel after having lived through the most intense, useful, important and glorious days of my life, when this courtroom seemed too small to hold all of the truths spoken, and we watched them squirming with impotence as they fought to hide each and every one of those truths.

And if an apology will make them happy, then I will offer them one: I am very sorry that I was unable to tell their agents that I was cooperating with the Cuban government. If they had an honest stance towards terrorism, I could have done so, and together we could have found a solution to the problem. When I think of those endless discussions about the specific intent to break the law, I realize that this situation goes far beyond the question of whether failing to register oneself is illegal or not. And that is because, unfortunately, even if foreign agents could advertise in the yellow pages here without being registered beforehand, we, being Cubans, would have to remain incognito for such basic tasks as neutralizing terrorists or drug traffickers, something we should be doing together, if a logical approach could prevail. I am also sorry if the anti-Castro affiliation of the criminals I fought brought them closer to certain officials or members of the Attorney General's Office. I feel very badly about this, honestly.

Actually, this whole issue of Cuban agents has a very simple solution: Leave Cuba alone. Do your job. Respect the sovereignty of the Cuban people. I would gladly send every last spy back to the island. We have better things to do there, all of them a lot more constructive than watching the criminals who freely walk the streets of Miami.

I do not want to pass up this opportunity to address myself to the many good people we have had the chance to meet during this trial.

First of all, I want to thank the U.S. Marshals for their professional behavior, their decency, their courtesy and their anonymous sacrifice. There were times when we good-naturedly sympathized with each other for being the only people in the courtroom whose needs were not taken into account in the time schedules, and we all laughed together about it. But they were always disciplined and did their duties well.

I also want to thank the translators, Larry, Richard and Lisa. They did a first-class job and were always available whenever our families or we needed their services. I offer them my sincerest gratitude for their hard work and decency towards everyone. It must be a privilege for this court to have a team like them. My best wishes to Mr. Londergan as well.

I also wish to extend my deepest respect to the members of the U.S. military who testified, whether for the prosecution or the defense, and who spoke sincerely, as well as to the officials, experts and agents who were honest. I would have liked to see more honesty among the latter group, and I would have gladly acknowledged it here.

To all of them, who could very well represent the best of the American people, I extend my highest regards and my assurances that there is an entire nation of people just a step to the south from here who do not harbor the slightest animosity towards their big northern neighbor. Individuals who either do not know, or do not want to know, or are not interested in knowing what Cuba really is have, systematically slandered those people, and that country, throughout this trial. I am going to take the liberty of reading an excerpt from a letter written by my wife on July 30:

"René, there are constant shows of support here for us, the families, and for all of you. Yesterday, when I took bus 58 home from Mom's house, a number of people recognized me, and Yvette was talking to everyone. Because it's carnival time, the bus filled right up when we went through Centro Habana, and Yvette decided to act up when it was time for us to get off; she sat herself down on the stairs of the bus and refused to get up. You can imagine what it was like, the bus full of people, me bouncing around trying to pick her up and not being able to, Yvette glued to her spot and everyone pushing. Then a woman came up to me; she squeezed my hand and gave me a prayer card she had suddenly pulled out of her purse, entitled, "A Happy Home". And she said, 'At my church we pray for the five every day, and we pray for their children to have a happy home, like Jesus did, because they were over there so that all children would have a happy home as well.'

"She kind of caught me by surprise, I almost didn't have time to thank her because I had to get off the bus quickly, but I realized that this is the way we Cubans are. And today we are more united than ever, regardless of beliefs or religions, everyone with their own faith, but all united in the same cause. I am going to keep the prayer card as a memento."

I feel obliged to stop reading here to clarify that I am not a religious person. I do not want the prosecution to distort my words later and claim that I have brought God into this courtroom out of hypocrisy.

Your Honor:

As you can see, even to talk about Cuba I do not need to air my political beliefs here. Others have done it in the framework of this trial throughout three years, oozing irrational hatred. And this hatred is even more absurd when you realize that it has been bred at a gut level, that it is a visceral hatred aimed at something that they simply do not know. It is truly sad to be taught to hate something that you do not even know.

And so there have been people here speaking with impunity against Cuba, offending a nation of people whose only crime is having chosen their own path, and having defended that choice successfully, at the cost of enormous sacrifices. I am not going to give anyone the benefit of distracting myself with all the lies told here about Cuba, but I will refer to one that was so monstrous as to amount to disrespect for this courtroom and the jury:

When Mr. Kastrenakes stood up and said, in front of this symbol of American justice, that we had come here to destroy the United States, he showed how little that symbol and that justice matter to him, and he also showed how little respect he had for the jury. Unfortunately, he was right with regard to the latter.

Neither the evidence in this case, or history, or our beliefs, nor the education we received supports the absurd idea that Cuba wants to destroy the United States. The problems of the human race cannot be resolved by destroying any country; for too many centuries, empires have been destroyed only for similar or worse empires to be built on their ruins. Any threat to this nation is not going to come from a people like the people of Cuba, where it is considered immoral to burn a flag, whether it is from the United States or any other country.

If you allow me, as a descendant of industrious and hard-working Americans, with the privilege of having been born in this country and the privilege of having grown up in

Cuba, I would tell the noble American people not to look so far to the south to find the threat to the United States.

Cling to the real and genuine values that inspired the founding fathers of this nation. The lack of these values, pushed aside by other less idealistic interests, is the real threat to this society. Power and technology can become a weakness if they are not in the hands of cultured people, and the hatred and ignorance we have seen here towards a small country, which nobody here knows, can be dangerous when combined with a blinding sense of power and false superiority. Go back to Mark Twain and forget about Rambo if you really want to leave your children a better country. Every alleged Christian who was brought up here to lie after swearing on the Bible is a threat to this country, in view of the way their conduct served to undermine these values.

Your Honor:

Having written these words in preparation for my sentencing, scheduled for September 26, the tragic and horrendous crimes of September 11 have obliged me to add a few reflections that I cannot fail to share with this Court. I must be very tactful, to ensure that nobody can accuse me of capitalizing on these abominable acts in my own favor. But there are times when we must speak certain truths, no matter how painful they may be. It is very much like telling a son or daughter, a brother or sister, when they have made a mistake, and we want, out of love, to help them avoid making that same mistake in the future. It is in that spirit

53

that I want to speak through you with this message to the American people.

The seeds of the tragedy that has plunged this nation into mourning today were sown many years ago. We were led to believe that by shooting down civilian planes and bombing schools, in a place as distant as it was unknown, certain individuals were fighting for freedom, simply because they were fighting communism. I would never blame the American people for that lack of vision; but those who provided the missiles and created an image of those people that did not match their criminal acts were also committing the crime of hypocrisy.

And I am not looking back into the past to rub it in anyone's face. I merely want to invite you to look at the present and reflect on the future, by sharing the following reflection with this court: "Yesterday's hypocrisy is to today's tragedy what today's hypocrisy will be to tomorrow's tragedy." We all have a responsibility towards our children, which goes beyond political prejudices or the petty need to earn a salary, hold on to an ephemeral political post or ingratiate ourselves with a handful of tycoons. That responsibility obliges us to put aside today's hypocrisy, so that we can give them a tomorrow free of tragedies.

They have sought to judge the five of us in the name of this hypocrisy, and now that it is my turn to face my sentence, I realize that, unlike my comrades, I do not even have the right to consider myself a victim. They way in which I conducted myself perfectly coincides with the description offered in the charges brought against me. If I have come to this trial, it is out of solidarity with my brothers, and in order to speak certain truths and refute the lies with which the prosecution tried to exaggerate my activities and present me as a danger to American society.

Therefore, I do not even have the right to ask for clemency at a moment like this, a moment at which this court will have seen who knows how many converts, some genuine, others false, some finding God after signing a pact with the Devil, all of them using this podium to show their repentance. I cannot judge them, and each will know what to do with his dignity. I also know what to do with mine, and I would like to believe that you would understand that I have no reason to repent.

Yet, I will always feel obliged to ask for justice for my comrades, accused of crimes they did not commit and sentenced on the basis of prejudices by a jury that passed up a unique opportunity to make a difference. They never attempted to obtain any secrets from this country, and as for the most monstrous accusation, it was merely a matter of a patriot defending the sovereignty of his nation. Quoting the words of a good Cuban and friend, who despite having come to this country for disagreeing with the Cuban government is still an honorable person, I want to take advantage of this moment to pay tribute to the worthy Cubans who live here as well, and to refute, along the way, another of the lies spread by the prosecution regarding our feelings towards the Cuban community: "Those boys were convicted for the crime of dignity."

Over two years ago, I received a letter from my father, in which he said, among other things, that he hoped a jury would be found in which the values of Washington,

Jefferson and Lincoln prevailed. It is shameful that he turned out to be wrong.

But I have not lost hope in the human race and its capacity to pursue those values. After all, I do not think that Washington, Jefferson and Lincoln themselves represented the majority during the era in which they left their mark on the history of this nation.

And as these three sordid years go down in history, and a mountain of arguments, motions and technicalities come to bury a story of blackmail, power abuse and the most absolute contempt for such a highly praised justice system, polished to a shine it never had, we will continue to appeal to those values, and to the American people's vocation for truth. And we will do so with all the patience, faith and courage that we draw from the crime of dignity.

Thank you very much.

René González Sehwerert

STATEMENT PRESENTED BY FERNANDO GONZÁLEZ LLORT AT THE SENTENCING HEARING

Tuesday, December 18, 2001

Your Honor:

I share with my comrades who have preceded me here in their recognition and gratitude for the professional behavior of Richard, the translators who have worked so efficiently, and the U.S. Marshals.

I also share in what has been expressed here by every one of my brothers at their sentencing hearings. I feel honored by the friendship of these comrades and brothers, who received their unjust sentences with such courage and dignity.

I also want to express my gratitude for the professional work of the attorneys representing the five of us, particularly Joaquín Méndez and the south Florida district public defenders office.

If it were not very clear to me that the fanaticism, hatred and irrationality felt towards Cuba are generated and stimulated by only a minority segment of the Cuban-

This marked the beginning of a long history of aggression against Cuba in every field of the country's economic and social life. A history in which economic warfare, biological warfare, and psychological warfare through propaganda and the threat of military attack, have combined with terrorism, sabotage, paramilitary actions and attempts on the lives of the political leaders of the Revolution, almost all of them originating in south Florida.

The prosecution will say that this is just Cuba's propaganda and paranoia. I wonder if they would have the nerve to go to Cuba and say that to the mothers, spouses and children of those who have lost their lives as victims of these acts of aggression. Such statements on the part of the prosecution demonstrate their lack of human sensitivity and their inability to put themselves in someone else's shoes.

The activities of the Cuban-American terrorist and paramilitary groups based in South Florida have been used as instruments of this country's foreign policy towards Cuba through their direct organization by U.S. government agencies, the support given by these agencies to the extremist groups that perpetrate the acts, or by simply allowing them to operate without real persecution or with benevolent treatment when someone has actually been arrested.

The terrorist groups of the Miami Cuban ultra-right wing were created, trained and financed by the CIA. This has always been abundantly clear to the Cuban people. If there are still any doubts among those present in this courtroom, they need merely take a look at the documents declassified by the United States government itself in 1997 and 1998, which clearly expose the decisions adopted by this country's top leaders.

One of these documents refers to a meeting attended by high-level officials, headed up by the vice president at the time, Richard Nixon. This was the meeting at which the so-called "Program of Covert Action Against the Castro Regime" was approved. In a memorandum on the meeting, one of the participants, General Goodpaster, noted, "The President said that he knows of no better plan for dealing with this situation. The great problem is leakage and breach of security. Everyone must be prepared to swear that he (Eisenhower) has not heard of it. (...) He said our hand should not show in anything that is done."

I ask myself: what can we expect 30 or 40 years from now, when they decide to declassify documents on what is happening today?

The majority of Cuban-Americans who remain active in terrorist actions against Cuba today, 40 years later, are well known to the United States security agencies, because they belong to those agencies, and have learned everything they know about technical means and working methods from them.

Their ties with the far right fundamentalists of U.S. politics have led to their apparent involvement in the darkest episodes of this country's recent history: the assassination of President Kennedy, the Watergate scandal, the murders of Orlando Letelier and Ronnie Moffit, and the clandestine supply of arms to the Nicaraguan Contras, in violation of the laws passed by Congress. Their activities have always run counter to the interests of the American people.

terrorists is being arranged, while conditions are created for an eventual escape. There is no need to add that here, on the radio and in the press controlled by the Cubans of the far right, they are considered patriots, and not lowly terrorists, which is what they really are.

All of this is taking place in full view of this country's authorities.

A lengthy account could be given of the entire terrorist and paramilitary activities and the attempts on the lives of Cuba's political leaders organized from south Florida. With regard to the latter, in 1975 the Church Commission of the U.S. Senate compiled a partial list of those in which the CIA was directly involved, and for which it even resorted to members of organized crime. Such is their lack of ethics.

What choice do the Cuban people have for defending their sovereignty and their security?

All of us here in this courtroom are familiar with the concept of "probable cause", used, among other things, for authorizing the use of certain means and methods in criminal investigations, for carrying out searches, making arrests, and so on. Who in the U.S. government can state here in this courtroom that over these last 42 years, there has not been "probable cause" to justify and legally support the investigation of actions initiated or financed from south Florida against Cuba?

In the course of our trial, the prosecution, in a blatant show of hypocrisy, threatened to use the R.I.C.O. Act against witnesses for the defense if they testified in this courtroom. Their goal was to keep the terrorist activities in which these gentlemen had participated from coming to light.

The R.I.C.O. Act, passed by Congress fundamentally to fight organized crime, has been in force for over 20 years. However, it has never been applied to a single one of the terrorist groups based here in Miami, although the government has all the information required to do so.

Here you have an example that there are in fact laws that would allow for these individuals and groups to be criminally prosecuted.

The problem is that, at the very least, there has been no political will to do so. If that political will did exist, many of the terrorist organizations that publicly operate offices in Miami would have been forced to shut down and their members sent to prison.

This is just a brief summary of the reality that the Cuban people have had to face and with which they have had to live throughout more than 40 years. The Cuban people have the right to defend themselves, because up until now the U.S. government, which is responsible for enforcing the laws of this country and passing new laws if they are needed to combat criminal acts, has done very little or nothing to stop these activities against Cuba.

It was within this context that we reached the decade of the 90s. Cuba was facing the most critical economic situation in the last 40 years, fundamentally as a result of external factors.

The terrorist groups based in Miami and allied with the far right of U.S. politics believed that the time had come to deal the definitive coup de grâce to Cuba's revolutionary

He was a guest on the same radio station, with the same host and on the same show normally used to raise funds for actions against Cuba, for the defense of terrorists, and as a forum for anti-Cuban propaganda and political activity characterized by fanaticism.

That is where this FBI special agent appeared.

It is striking that in his comments and explanations to the public about the supposed activities of agents working for the Cuban government in south Florida, there is no mention of anything related to the national security of the United States. There is, however, acknowledgement of the fact that there are groups here in Miami plotting to overthrow the Cuban government. This violates the Neutrality Act, although it is clear that this issue was not brought up during the show.

On that very same radio show, this FBI agent acknowledged that actions and attacks against the Cuban government are perpetrated from Miami, and that the goal of the Cuban government is to remain informed of these plans. To top it all, the FBI agent bid farewell to his listeners by informing them that "we are fighting and we have the same objectives: for Cuba to be free as soon as possible."

As far as I know, the FBI was not created to fight for the freedom of any other country, nor is this one of its functions. However, these statements clearly highlight the political agenda of the FBI office in south Florida.

Coincidentally, these statements were made in October of 1990, precisely at the beginning of a decade in which terrorist acts against Cuba from south Florida would be stepped up considerably.

Statements like these, coming from an FBI agent and made on a radio station show with the above-mentioned characteristics, could only serve to encourage the organizers of terrorist acts against Cuba and offer them the security that they will not be persecuted for their actions.

Mr. Héctor Pesquera, the agent in charge of the south Florida FBI office, appeared as a guest on the same station, the same show, and with the same host, just days after the verdict was announced in our trial.

In the face of these realities, what can Cuba do to defend itself and be forewarned of terrorist plans?

Can the authorities of the south Florida FBI be trusted when it comes to matters related to Cuba's national security?

Can someone who is here to look into the activities of terrorist groups and to prevent their actions in order to deter the death of innocent people be officially registered with the U.S. government?

What can Cuba do to defend its people, when boats leaving Florida loaded with weapons to attack Cuba are seized by the U.S. authorities, and those authorities are satisfied with explanations like, "We're lobster fishing"? We heard this in this very courtroom from an ATF agent who intercepted a boat loaded with weapons and maps of Cuba just 40 miles off its coasts.

On July 23, 1998, the *Miami Herald* reported comments made by terrorist Tony Bryant, who laughed over how he was questioned by FBI officials after his boat was found near Havana with explosives on board. According to what Bryant told the newspaper, he promised he would not do it again, and they let him go.

Later that night, in that same speech, President Bush stated:

"We will come together to strengthen our intelligence capabilities, to know the plans of terrorists before they act and to find them before they strike."

Cuba, which has suffered terrorist attacks for 42 years, also has the right to defend itself in this way. Today, the American nation has joined in the fight against terrorism, something that has been a necessity and a reality for my country for many years.

There can be no double standards. Terrorism must be combated and eliminated whether it is committed against a big and powerful country or against small countries. There is no such thing as bad terrorism and good terrorism.

In the report on Orlando Bosh submitted in 1989 by Undersecretary of Justice Joe D. Whitley, whose administrative position made him less subject to political pressures or foreign policy considerations, this U.S. government official stated:

"The United States cannot tolerate the inherent inhumanity of terrorism as a way of settling disputes. Appeasement of those who would use force will only breed more terrorists. We must look on terrorism as a universal evil, even if it is directed toward those with whom we have no political sympathy."

Your Honor:

Today, you will conclude this stage of our trial and pronounce the sentence that you deem appropriate.

Finally, I simply want to reiterate that at no time did I endanger the national security of the United States, nor was this ever my intent, or that of my comrades.

What I did was inspired by love for my country, and by the conviction that history will register that this is the only choice left to the Cuban people to prevent the death of innocent people and the destruction wrought by the terrorist acts committed against my country.

It is up to the U.S. government to bring an end to these acts. Cuba has shown its willingness to cooperate with the U.S. authorities in this and other areas, like drug trafficking. This would serve the best interests of both nations, since it does affect the national security of the United States.

It is the authorities of this country that must decide to act on the basis of principles, and to shake off the destructive influence of a small but economically powerful group of mobsters and ultra-right fanatics from the Cuban community in Miami.

I sincerely trust that one day Cuba will have no need for people like me to come to this country, voluntarily and out of love for their country and their people, to fight against terrorism.

The first duty of any self-respecting person is to his or her country. Throughout the years of my imprisonment, I will always carry with me the dignity I have learned from my people and their history.

Thank you very much.

Fernando González Llort

STATEMENT PRESENTED BY ANTONIO GUERRERO RODRÍGUEZ AT THE SENTENCING HEARING

Wednesday, December 27, 2001

> Now on this spot
> I stand with my robust soul.
>
> Walt Whitman
> (From "Song of Myself")

Your Honor,

Allow me to say that I share everything that has been said in this courtroom by my four brothers in arms: Gerardo Hernández, Ramón Labaniño, René González and Fernando González. They spoke with dignity and courage to the Court. Our speeches are based on the strictest truth, on the soundness of the principles we embrace and in the honor of the heroic Cuban people. It is only fair to say that the

75

lawyers and their assistants acted in a highly professional, honest and courageous manner and that the translators, Liza, Richard and the marshals worked in a very ethical and professional way.

At the beginning I wrote in my diary of my long days, "… a real man does not look to see on which side one lives best, but on which side lies duty". Those are José Martí's words, which a century after they were written still encourage, live and are the essence of what is most pure and altruistic.

It is often difficult
To find the exact words,
But these have been in me
Beaten
Shaken
Incubated by the truth,
Waiting to break the shell and see the light.
And the day has come.
Allow me to explain my reasons, your Honor, in the clearest and most concise way:
Cuba,
My little country, has been
Attacked,
Assaulted,
And slandered
Decade after decade
By a cruel
Inhuman and absurd
Policy.
A real terrorist war,

Fierce and open,
The harbinger of horror
Of sabotage,
A ruin, murder maker
A grief carrier,
Of the most profound grief,
Death.

This aggression has been exposed not only by documents and information from the Cuban government but also by secret documents that the very government of the United States has declassified.

This aggression has included the CIA's recruiting, financing and training counterrevolutionary agents; the Bay of Pigs Invasion; Operation Mongoose; pretexts for military intervention; plans to assassinate heads of State and Government; infiltrations by armed groups; sabotage; violations of our airspace; spy flights, spraying with bacteriological and chemical agents; machine gun fire on our coasts and buildings; bombs in hotels and other social, cultural, historic and tourist centers, all kinds of cruel and vicious acts of provocation.

And the outcome of these acts:

More than three thousand four hundred dead; more than two thousand people left totally or partially handicapped; substantial damage to the economy, the source of our livelihood; hundreds of thousands of Cubans who are born and grow up under a harsh blockade and in a hostile cold war climate. Terror, hardships and pain have been brought over the entire population.

Where have such unceasing ruthless acts been hatched and financed?

For the most part, in the United States of America.

What has the government of this country done to avoid them?

Practically nothing.... And the aggression has not ceased...

Today, people who are responsible for some of these actions still walk freely the streets of Miami. And radio stations and other media give coverage to and instigate new acts of aggression against the Cuban people.

Why so much hatred for the Cuban people?

Is it because Cuba chose a different road?

Because its people want socialism?

Because it did away with the large estates

and wiped out illiteracy?

Because it gave free education

and medical care to its people?

Because it lets

the dawn break freely over its children?

Cuba has never placed the security of the United States in jeopardy nor committed any act of aggression or terrorism against it. It deeply loves peace and quiet and wants the best relations between our two countries. It has shown that it admires and respects the American people.

"Cuba is not a military threat to the United States," Admiral Carroll said in this courtroom.

General Atkinson testified that Cuba presents "zero" military threat to the United States.

It is my country's unquestionable right — like that of any other — to defend itself against those who try to harm its people.

The job of putting a stop to these terrorist acts has been complex and difficult because the terrorists have enjoyed the complicity or lax tolerance of the authorities.

My country has done everything possible to warn the US government of the danger of these acts and to do so it has used official, unofficial and public channels. However, such cooperation has never been reciprocated.

In the nineties, fired up by the demise of the socialist camp, terrorist groups intensified their activities against Cuba. It was, they felt, the long dreamed hour for stirring up the final chaos, for terrorizing the people, destabilizing the economy, damaging the tourist industry, building up a crisis and dealing the death blow to the Cuban Revolution.

What could Cuba do to defend itself and be forewarned of the terrorist plans against it? What could it do to avoid a greater conflict? What options did it have to safeguard its sovereignty and the safety of its children?

One way to prevent these brutal and bloody acts, to prevent the suffering becoming worse because of more deaths was to move quietly.

There was no alternative but to rely on men who –out of love for a just cause, out of love for their country and their people, out of love for peace and life– were prepared to voluntarily agree to carry out this honorable duty against terrorism, that is, to give advanced warning of the danger of attack.

The reason behind my acts and the motive for doing my duty, the same as my comrades', has been to prevent a conflict that would bring sorrow to our peoples.

We were not moved to do what we did by money or resentment. It did not occur to any of us to harm the noble and hard-working American people. We did nothing detrimental to the national security of the United States. The court records show it. Those who doubt my words may examine them and find the truth.

The barbaric attacks on the World Trade Center and the Pentagon last September 11 filled with indignation everyone who loves a peaceful world. The unexpected and unwonted deaths of thousand of this country's innocent citizens pierced our hearts with deep sorrow.

Nobody can deny that terrorism is an inhuman, ruthless and repugnant phenomenon that must be eliminated with the utmost urgency.

"And in order to make sure that we're able to conduct a winning victory, we've got to have the best intelligence we can possibly have." "Unity is needed to strengthen the intelligence agencies, so that we can learn what the plans are before they are implemented and to discover the terrorists before they attack."

These two statements were not made by the president of the Republic of Cuba, our Commander in Chief Fidel Castro, but by the president of the United States, after these horrendous attacks. I have wondered over and over again. Are these statements not valid for Cuba, which is a victim of terrorism?

This is exactly what Cuba has done to try to put an end to this scourge, which has also buffeted her territory for so many years and made martyrs of her people.

Your Honor,

A "trial" took place
This courtroom knows as much,
We lived together and we lived through days full of statements
Testimony,
Circumstantial evidence,
Evidence,
Arguments,
Motions,
Commitments,
Doubts,
Slanderous allegations,
Falsehoods,
Deliberations,
I didn't come here today to justify anything,
I came to tell
The truth:
"That is the only thing I am committed to."
Accord; there was none except the commitment to be useful to the world, to serve a valid cause called humanity and also motherland.
Intent, there was none except to prevent senselessness and crime and to save the living flower from chance, sudden, pointless and premature death.

There was no transgression and no offense. Nobody was insulted.

Nothing was stolen. No one was deceived. No one was cheated.

No one tried to or practiced espionage.

Nobody ever asked me to get any classified information. Here in this courtroom the witnesses' statements confirmed that, not only defense witnesses but also those of the prosecution itself.

Read General Clapper's, Joseph Santos' and General Atkinson's testimony, to name but a few, and they will confirm what I say in all honesty.

And many other people could have come to this court to explain things about my life, to say what I did every day just as Dalila Borrego, Edward Donohue, and Tim Carey came. On the other hand, nobody came here to speak against me, nor would it be possible to find anyone who, in all sincerity, could point to any failing in my conduct in this society.

I love the island where I grew up, where I was educated and where my mother, one of my beloved children, many of the people I love and many of my other friends live. I also love this country where I was born, where, over the last ten years, I have given and received real proof of love and solidarity.

I am certain that a bridge of friendship will definitely be laid not only between these two peoples but also among all the peoples in the world.

It falls to you, your Honor, to hand down sentence in this long and tortuous trial.

Bring proof and evidence together!

Voices will say that they don't exist.
Take into account facts and arguments!
Voices will say they carry no weight:
Read cases and testimony!
Voices will say it is not possible
To blame these men.
Voices that arise from the heart itself.
Voices inspired by the strength of justice.
Voices which did not want to be, or which were not
Listened to by a jury
Which could not serve justice.

They were wrong! Their verdict was sacrilege. But we were aware, from the beginning, that when it comes to Cuba, Miami is an impossible place for justice.

This has been, above all else, a political trial.

Personally, I ask for nothing else but justice; for the good of our countries, for the sake of truth. A fair, full sentence, free from political strings, would have sent an important message in this crucial moment in the fight against terrorism.

Allow me to repeat that I have never caused personal harm to anyone not have caused any property damage. I have never tried to take any action, which would endanger the national security of the United States.

If I were asked to do the same thing again, I would do it with honor. An excerpt from a letter that Cuban general Antonio Maceo, who fought for Cuban independence in the 19th century, wrote to a Spanish general comes to mind at this time with force and passion:

"I shall not find any reasons for having cut myself off from humanity. I pursue not a policy of hatred but of love; this is not an exclusionist policy but one founded in human morality".

Because of your rulings, my beloved brothers and I must be unjustly kept in prison, but there we shall not cease from defending the cause and the principles we have embraced.

The day will come when we will not have to live under the shadow of fear and death, and on that historic day, the true justice of our cause will be seen.

Your Honor,

Many days and months of an unjust, cruel and horrible imprisonment have gone by!

I have sometimes wondered, what is time? And like Saint Agustin I have answered myself, "If they ask me I don't know, but if they don't ask me, I do know." Hours of solitude and hopes, of reflection about injustice and small mindedness; eternal minutes in which memories burn bright: There are memories that burn the memory!

I take these verses by Martí for this last page that I write in the diary of my long days:

"I have lived:
It was to duty that I pledged my arms
And not once did the sun drop down behind the hills
That did not see my struggle and my victory..."

(Free verses)

And here in this courtroom I quote from the Uruguayan and world poet, Mario Benedetti:

84

"...victory will be there, just like me,
simply germinating"

Because, in the end, we shall rest free and victorious beneath that sun which we are denied today.

Thank you.

Antonio Guerrero

THE FIVE HEROES IMPRISONED BY THE EMPIRE

On January 1, 1959, upon the triumph of the Cuban Revolution, the government of the United States of America welcomed some of the most notorious murderers of the Fulgencio Batista dictatorship into its territory with open arms; that dictatorship had claimed the lives of close to 20,000 Cubans during almost seven years of bloody repression. Within the space of barely a few days, these criminal ranks had spawned in U.S. territory the first of hundreds of counterrevolutionary organizations, which have resorted to every means possible in the attempt to destroy the social project undertaken on the island throughout four decades.

In the 43 years that have passed since that time, alongside the genocidal blockade and the economic war that successive U.S. administrations have waged against Cuba to asphyxiate the country and bring its people to their knees through hunger and disease, and all of the absurd laws and amendments adopted to inflict damage on the island, there have been literally thousands of terrorists acts committed against our nation, with the consent, financing or knowledge of the U.S. authorities and intelligence services, by the

Cuban-American mafia, headquartered in Miami. Many of the principal figures in this mafia were trained by the CIA in the 1960s and 1970s to organize acts of sabotage and aggression of every kind. Such ignominious actions against our people have cost the lives of 3478 Cuban citizens and left another 2099 physically disabled.

Dozens of armed gangs supplied from abroad, mercenary invasions, explosions and fires provoked in industries, businesses and recreational facilities, bombs planted in Cuban offices abroad, the murder of Cuban diplomatic personnel abroad, the burning of sugar cane fields, the introduction of plagues, viruses and diseases, gunfire on coastal settlements and tourism facilities, hundreds of attempts on the lives of the principal leaders of the Revolution, particularly Fidel Castro, armed infiltrations and the planting of bombs in major hotels: these are all a part of the long list of terrorist acts perpetrated against Cuba.

Among so many abhorrent actions, we could point specifically to the criminal attack on the French ship La Coubre, which led to the death of 101 people, including six French sailors; the mercenary invasion of the Bay of Pigs, defeated in less than 72 hours; the CIA's Operation Mongoose, comprising the most diverse array of anti-Cuban activities and leading to the establishment of the largest substation in the Agency's history; the blowing up in midair of a Cubana Airlines plane off the coast of Barbados in 1976, in which 73 people were killed – 57 Cubans, 11 Guyanese and five Koreans; the introduction of a hemorrhagic dengue epidemic in 1981, which affected

344,203 people and cost the lives of 158, of whom 101 were children; and over 600 assassination plots hatched against President Fidel Castro.

The violent acts against our country were significantly stepped up in the decade of the 1990s. Spurred on by the fall of the eastern European socialist camp and the disappearance of the Soviet Union, and dreaming of the rapid demise of the Cuban Revolution, the Miami terrorist mafia executed over 200 actions against Cuba in those ten years. Tourism facilities were particularly targeted, given that tourism had become the main source of support for an economy that had lost 85% of its foreign trade overnight and was facing severe difficulties as a consequence. The terrorist methods used against the island in the last decade have been wide-ranging: gunfire on hotels in Varadero and Cayo Coco; a wave of explosions in five hotels in Havana in 1997; the infiltration of heavily armed individuals from Miami, for the purpose of planting explosives in well-known and popular tourist attractions like the world-famous Tropicana cabaret – the most recent of these groups was captured in April 2001; and even the threat of blowing up planes carrying tourists to Cuba from other Latin American countries.

An active role in these heinous activities has been played by the Cuban-American National Foundation (CANF), which operates under the cover of a "humanitarian foundation" to organize and finance major criminal actions against our country, including the majority of those perpetrated in the 1990s. It also lobbies Congress to promote sanctions and laws against the island and finances the campaigns of U.S. politicians opposed to relations of any kind with Cuba.

The CANF is the principal source of financing for the exploits of Luis Posada Carriles, one of the world's most notorious terrorists. Together with Orlando Bosch, he was one of the masterminds behind the blowing up of the plane over Barbados, and the organizer of the series of explosions in Havana hotels previous to and during the celebration in the Cuban capital of the 14th World Festival of Youth and Students in 1997, which brought together over 13,000 young people from some 100 countries around the globe. Posada Carriles has been in prison in Panama for over a year now, awaiting trial for a plot to assassinate Cuban President Fidel Castro during the Ibero-American Summit in 2000; had his plans come to fruition, they could have cost the lives of thousands of Panamanian students or numerous heads of state from our region.

In view of this ongoing and relentless aggression, and given the brazen impunity with which these terrorist elements walk the streets of Miami, where they plan and finance their brutal actions, coupled with the inaction or consent of the U.S. authorities, Cuba has the right to implement all of the measures within its reach to protect the lives of its people, the lives of citizens of other nations who visit our country, and even the people of the United States itself from terrorist acts of this kind.

The anti-Cuban criminal mafia has perpetrated hundreds of terrorist acts on U.S. soil against institutions or individuals connected to Cuba or supportive of normal relations with our country. They have planted bombs in popular public venues in Miami, like the Centro Vasco; freely shot down Luciano Nieves, a Cuban-American *proponent of peaceful coexistence with Cuba; murdered former Chilean foreign minister Orlando Letelier and his American secretary Ronni Moffitt by blowing up his car on the streets of Washington; and publicly burned in Miami a famous painting, "The Peacock", by renowned Cuban artist Manuel Mendive, in addition to many other acts of vandalism, which genuinely threaten the peace of the American people and the national security of the United States.*

Today, when the nightmarish images of the horrific terrorist attack on New York's Twin Towers are still fresh in our minds, it would be good to look back at September 11, 1980, the day that Félix García Rodríguez, a Cuban diplomat accredited before the United Nations, was killed in broad daylight on a busy New York street by agents of this murderous mafia. His killers have yet to be punished.

In view of this "state of necessity" to defend the lives of its people, the Cuban Revolution has been obliged to implement a variety of measures. These have included seeking information from within the terrorist groups themselves; this strategy, of course, is very much a part of the new anti-terrorist plans adopted by U.S. intelligence agencies after the events of September 11.

On numerous occasions, Cuba has shared the information it has gathered on the plans of these organizations with officials from the Federal Bureau of Investigations. In June of 1998, our country provided a high-level FBI delegation with thick files and audio and video cassette recordings documenting the terrorist plans and actions of the Miami mafia. These officials promised to take action based on the evidence handed over by Cuba.

The bizarre action consequently taken by the FBI was the arrest on September 12, 1998, some three months later, of a group of Cubans who had infiltrated various counterrevolutionary organizations to gather information on their plans for aggression against Cuba and send that information back to their country, for the sole purpose of frustrating these terrorist acts aimed at sowing panic, suffering and death among the Cuban people.

Since then, five courageous young Cubans have been subjected to unjust, humiliating and harsh imprisonment in U.S. jails, when the only crimes they are guilty of are patriotism and dignity. They have been forced to bear the full brunt of the thirst for revenge and visceral hatred of the terrorist mafia, fully defeated in its policy and actions of constant hostility against the Cuban nation, furious over the international prestige earned by Cuba, fearful of the ever growing number of voices within important sectors of U.S. society speaking out against the White House's absurd policy towards Cuba, particularly concerning the blockade, and repudiated and crushed after its criminal and despicable kidnapping of little Elián González Brotóns.

Throughout 17 long months, these heroic men were kept locked up in a special housing unit (SHU), commonly known among prisoners as "the hole". During that time, three of them were not allowed contact of any kind with their families or their country. A fourth was allowed no more than a glimpse of his daughters – one of them barely a year old -- from the windows of the Federal Detention Center in Miami.

Despite such brutal treatment, however, nothing could break the spirit and integrity of these men.

At the time of their arrest, the affidavit presented by the FBI on September 15, 1998 accused them of conspiracy and of being foreign agents. When these charges were put forward in court in October of 1998, the prosecution accused them of conspiracy, conspiracy to commit espionage, of being unauthorized foreign agents, and of possession of forged documents. Almost eight months later, in May of 1999, a new bill of indictment was presented, including a charge against one of the defendants of conspiracy to commit murder. This charge resulted from the shameless attempt to connect him to the events of February 24, 1996, in which two planes from the Brothers to the Rescue terrorist organization were shot down after repeatedly violating Cuban airspace. What was truly striking was the fact that this new list of charges was announced by the Miami press even before it was made official by the prosecution. This manipulation of the charges against the five, closely linked to the mafia's attempts to steal a large chunk of funds – through another trial underway at the time – from the Cuban financial assets frozen in U.S. banks as a result of the blockade, demonstrated from the very beginning the political nature this trial would have.

On November 27, 2000, with the jury selection process, the blatantly rigged trial of these five Cuban patriots began. On December 6 of that same year, the oral proceedings were initiated. Over the course of seven months, testimony was offered by expert witnesses and witnesses for the prosecution and witnesses for the defense.

The case put forward by the prosecution was inconsistent and lacking in evidence, with testimony given by blatantly manipulated expert witnesses and witnesses of such low moral caliber as Rodolfo Frómeta, the top leader of the counterrevolutionary organization Comandos F-4, who brazenly boasted of his repeated attempts to assassinate President Fidel Castro under the complacent regard of the prosecutors.

The poor performance of the prosecution, typical of a "fixed" trial with clearly political ends, was so obvious that even the mafia's mouthpiece, the Spanish-language daily El Nuevo Heraldo, printed a commentary on March 2, 2001 by Ernesto Betancourt, former director of the misnamed anti-Cuban radio station Radio Martí, who harshly criticized the performance of the prosecution and the unexpected turn taken by the trial: "It seems as if the accused are no longer the spies, and the Cuban-American community, particularly the Brothers to Rescue, are the ones actually being put on trial."

On the other hand, the defense attorneys, who were the assigned counsel, managed to put forward through their witnesses overwhelming proof of the integrity of each one of the defendants, the complete lack of danger posed to national security, the lengthy terrorist record of the anti-Cuban mafia, the illegitimacy of the charge of conspiracy to commit murder, and the complicity of certain U.S. authorities with this mafia. The defense called on important political figures to testify, including Richard Nuccio, who served as former President Clinton's Cuban advisor, and such highly placed military figures as General Charles

Wilhelm, former chief of the Southern Command, who expressed his conviction that Cuba did not constitute a threat to the United States and that these young men had not harmed that country's national security.

The defense even succeeded in calling, as a hostile witness, José Basulto, the leader of the counterrevolutionary organization Brothers to the Rescue, who was clearly unmasked as the terrorist and mobster that he is and for his efforts to provoke tension between Cuba and the United States. This was such a devastating blow that the prosecution threatened other agents of the Miami mafia called on to testify that if they did not plead the Fifth Amendment and thus remain silent, they would be tried for involvement in organized crime. This was the kind of "clean" behavior demonstrated by the prosecution.

The overwhelming evidence put forward by the defense – which included videotaped depositions by Cuban expert witnesses and witnesses – and the strength of the arguments they wielded led the Miami mafia and its radio, television and printed press mouthpieces to launch a call to the anti-Cuban community, warning of the danger of losing the trial and spewing diatribes about what was happening in the court, thus creating an atmosphere of blatant pressure around the proceedings. On May 17, 2001, near the end of the oral proceedings, the libelous Nuevo Heraldo itself published an article entitled "Prosecution fears a conspiracy against it".

On numerous occasions, the defense put forward motions to the federal judge in charge of the case requesting a change in venue for the trial, to a city other than Miami, *where the atmosphere was so clearly hostile and biased, where the anti-Cuban mafia regularly buys off judges and prosecutors, the media, the police, politicians and the FBI, where a minority imposes its aggressive anti-Cuban agenda on a silent majority. But all of these requests were denied.*

As a result, in spite of what happened during the 103 sessions of the trial, it came as no surprise when on June 8, 2001, without a single question or doubt regarding the endless issues addressed in these lengthy proceedings, the testimony of 90 witnesses and expert witnesses, or the mountain of evidence put forward, the jury in this machiavellian trial declared the five accused to be guilty of all charges against them. Once again, U.S. justice proved to be blind, deaf and dumb.

But injustice did not lead these men to be disheartened. Evidence of this is provided by a letter written by Gerardo Hernández, who was accused of the most serious charges, to his wife, two days after the jury announced its verdict. "I feel very serene," he said, "with the serenity you get when you feel you are innocent, when your conscience is clean, and you know you are the victim of injustice. I am confident that the truth will win out someday, and justice will be done, but even if that is not the case, because I know that sometimes it isn't easy, you can rest assured that I will always feel the same way. When you have a cause to fight for, a people to defend, a family that supports you, and a person you love, and who loves you back; when you know that you can't let them down, you can face up to anything, no matter how difficult it is, with all the serenity and dignity in the world."

96

On June 20, 2001, a message was issued from the five Cuban patriots to the people of the United States, in which they explain the reasons for their presence in that country and emphasize that it was never their intent to harm this noble people. In their letter, they say, "We are the victims of a terrible injustice [...] We can say, without the shadow of a doubt, that neither with our attitude nor our actions have we in any way interfered with, or jeopardized the security of, the American people. What we have certainly done is contribute to exposing terrorist plans and actions against our people [...] The defendants in this trial are in no way repentant of what we have done to defend our country. We declare ourselves non guilty

From that day forward, the Cuban people have been waging an extraordinary battle to have these five brothers freed, a battle of ideas that is fought in televised debates on the Round Table program, in Open Forums in different municipalities throughout the country, and in patriotic marches past the U.S. Interests Section in Havana. More than a million Havana residents marched past this U.S. mission as part of a massive patriotic protest on July 26, 2001.

Solidarity groups calling for the release of these five political prisoners have sprung up in U.S. cities like New York, Los Angeles and Miami, as well as in Argentina, Bolivia, Uruguay, the Dominican Republic, Italy, France, the United Kingdom and other countries.

As an initial reaction to their message to the American people and the determined battle undertaken by the Cuban people, the five men were moved once again to the cells of the SHU, the "hole", where they spent close to two months. They were later separated and taken to cells on different floors and in different wings of the Federal Detention Center in Miami.

On December 11, 2001, the sentencing hearings against our five brave compatriots began. In hearings that lasted until December 27, Federal Judge Joan Leonard imposed the maximum sentence possible on each and every one of them. Gerardo Hernández was sentenced to two life sentences and 15 years; Ramón Labañino to a life sentence and 18 years; Antonio Guerrero to a life sentence and 10 years; Fernando González to 19 years; and René González to 15 years.

In the face of these outrageous sentences and the vile, shameful nature of the trial against them, these five heroic Cubans presented forceful statements on their own behalf at their sentencing trials, which shook the chambers of the Miami Federal Court. They raised their strong yet serene voices to harshly condemn all forms of terrorism, especially the terrorism perpetrated from Miami against Cuba over the last four decades. They denounced the despicable conduct of the anti-Cuban mafia, and the corrupt and treacherous behavior of the prosecution, the jury and the representatives of the FBI in southern Florida.

What was meant to be a trial against the Revolution, spurred on by its most bitter enemies, turned out to be yet another victory for our people. In its own lair, the mafia was forced to listen to countless truths in the voices of five men who did not use their opportunity to address the court to ask for clemency, but rather to denounce their despicable captors and proclaim their regret that they have but one life to give for their country.

The mafia and its mouthpieces have spent the past four years trying to discredit these men, disparagingly labeling them "dangerous spies". But what they have not said is that they are all brilliant young men, university graduates with excellent futures in their professions, who postponed their professional dreams and suffered separation from their families in order to devote their lives to defending their people from the criminal acts of a terrorist mafia capable of the most heinous crimes. The events of September 11 in the United States fully demonstrated the worthiness of the actions of these young men on behalf of security and world peace.

The example set by these five heroic men grows more lofty every day, making them formidable models of honor and principles for our young people, and young people around the world. The truths spoken by them in the "entrails of the monster" – to paraphrase José Martí – are the same truths held up by our people today in the colossal battle of ideas we are waging for a free, cultured and peaceful future for all our people and all humankind.

For having "fulfilled with exemplary dedication, dignity and steadfastness the sacred mission of defending the Homeland, and protecting it from terrorism, facing great risks to their lives and enduring enormous sacrifices in the most hostile, aggressive and corrupt setting possible," on December 29, 2001, in an extraordinary session, the National Assembly of People's Power decided, at the proposal of the President of the Council of State and Council of Ministers, to grant the Honorary Title of Heroes of the Republic of Cuba to Gerardo Hernández Nordelo, Ramón Labañino Salazar, Fernando González Llort, René González Sehwerert and Antonio Guerrero Rodríguez.

"Make way for those who are not afraid of the light…!"

RANDY ALONSO FALCÓN
January 21st, 2002

TRANSLATION
ESTI

DESIGN
Emilio Lamí

DIGITAL LAY-OUT
María del Carmen Remigio

This book was printed in Havana, Cuba,
in March, 2002,
"Year of the Heroes Imprisoned by the Empire"

Esta edición consta de 40 000 ejemplares